2
AGES 7-8

SCORE!
Mountain Challenge

MATH
WORKBOOK

KAPLAN

PUBLISHING

New York

Contributing Editor: Justin Serrano
Editorial Director: Jennifer Farthing
Editorial Development Manager: Tonya Lobato
Assistant Editor: Eric Titner
Production Editor: Dominique Polfliet
Production Artist: Creative Pages, Inc.
Cover Designer: Carly Schnur

Published by Kaplan Publishing, a division of Kaplan, Inc.
888 Seventh Ave.
New York, NY 10106

Printed in the United States of America

May 2007
10 9 8 7 6 5 4 3 2 1

ISBN-13: 978-1-4195-9454-0
ISBN-10: 1-4195-9454-0

Kaplan Publishing books are available at special quantity discounts to use for sales promotions, employee premiums, or educational purposes. Please email our Special Sales Department to order or for more information at kaplanpublishing@kaplan.com, or write to Kaplan Publishing, 888 Seventh Avenue, 22nd Floor, New York, NY 10106.

Table of Contents

How to Use Your *SCORE! Mountain*
Challenge Workbook . . . .**iv**

Time to Get Organized and
Learn to Use Your Time Wisely! . . . .**vii**

SCORE! Mountain Challenge
Online Instructions. . . . .**xii**

Base Camp 1: Number Sense **1**

Base Camp 2: Algebra **29**

Base Camp 3: Geometry. **57**

Base Camp 4: Probability and Statistics **85**

Base Camp 5: Interpreting Data **113**

Base Camp 6: Everyday Math **145**

Tools **175**

Are you ready for a fun and challenging trip up *SCORE!* Mountain?

Getting Started

This exciting, interactive workbook will guide you through 6 different base camps as you make your way up *SCORE!* Mountain. Along the way to the top you will get to challenge yourself with over 120 math activities and brain teasers.

To help you figure out the answer to each question, use the blank space on the page or the extra pages at the back of your workbook. If you need extra space, use a piece of scrap paper.

Base Camp

SCORE! Mountain is divided into 6 base camps—each covering an important math topic—and meets the educational standards set forth by the National Council of Teachers of Mathematics. The final base camp in this workbook, Everyday Math, has a special focus on the many ways we might use math each day.

Your trip through base camp will take you through 15 questions related to the base camp topic, a Challenge Activity designed to give your brain extra practice, and a 5-question test to see how much you've learned during your climb.

Each question comes with helpful hints to guide you to the right answer. Use these hints to make your climb up *SCORE!* Mountain a great learning experience!

The Answer Hider

Try your best to answer each quesion before looking at the answer. Included in the back of this workbook is a *SCORE!* answer hider that you can tear out. Use the answer hider to cover up the answers as you work on each question. Then, uncover the answer and see how well you did!

Celebrate!

At the end of each base camp, there's a fun celebration as a reward for making it through. It's your time to take a break before going to the next base camp!

SCORE! Mountain Challenge Online Companion

Don't forget—more fun awaits you online! Each base camp comes with a set of 10 online questions and activities, plus a mountain-climbing study partner who will encourage you and help you track your progress as you get closer to the top of *SCORE!* Mountain!

The *SCORE!* online base camps are designed to match the base camps from the workbook. As you reach the end of each base camp in this workbook, we encourage you to go to your computer to round out your *SCORE!* Mountain Challenge experience. Plus, after you successfully complete the last online base camp, you are awarded a Certificate of Achievement.

Certificate of Achievement

When you complete the entire workbook and online program, you will receive your very own Certificate of Achievement that can be shared with family and friends!

Time Management

In addition to all of the great math practice that your *SCORE! Mountain Challenge Workbook* has to offer, you'll find lots of helpful tips at the front of the workbook on how you can best organize your time so that you can do well at school, get all of your homework and chores done, and still have time for fun, family, and friends! It's a great way to help you perform at your best every day!

Tools

Every mountain climber needs a set of tools to help him/her reach the mountaintop! Your *SCORE! Mountain Challenge Workbook* has a special set of tools for you. In the back of your workbook you'll find a handy guide to help you get through each base camp. You can use these tools whenever you need a helping hand during your climb up *SCORE!* Mountain.

Enjoy your trip up *SCORE!* Mountain. We hope that it's a fun learning experience!

GOOD LUCK!

**Learning can be hard work!
Getting organized can help!**

General Skills

**It can be fun having a lot of things to do,
but sometimes we lose track of time!**

Keeping a schedule every week will help
you keep track of time.

If you make a schedule like this, you are sure not to
forget anything!

Sunday	Monday	Tuesday	Wednesday	Thursday	Friday	Saturday
1:00 Sara's Birthday Party	9:00-3:00 School 3:15 Soccer Practice 5:00 Homework	9:00-3:00 School 5:00 Homework	9:00-3:00 School 5:00 Homework 7:00 Special dinner with Mom	9:00-3:00 School 5:00 Homework	9:00-3:00 School 6:15 Play with Sam	10:00 Movie Day

Now it's your turn! What do you have to do each day of the week?

Sunday	Monday	Tuesday	Wednesday	Thursday	Friday	Saturday

Homework

Here are some helpful homework hints!

When doing homework:

- Turn off the television and keep the room quiet!
- Set up your homework space with a light.
- Keep all your books and materials neat and in order.
- Sometimes a small, healthful snack can help keep you going and energized!

It also helps to have a few items at your workspace:

- It helps to keep a dictionary, calculator, pencils, and extra paper handy.
- If you keep these items in a box near you, it makes learning a lot more organized and fun!

Try keeping a homework chart to help you remember all that you have to do.

Check off each item on the line when you're done!

Sunday	Monday	Tuesday	Wednesday	Thursday	Friday	Saturday
	Reading 20 minutes ✔ ___ Math problems 1–5 ___	Reading 20 minutes ___ Science reading Pages 10–14 ___	Reading 20 minutes ___	Reading 20 minutes ___ History worksheet ___		

Now it's your turn!

Sunday	Monday	Tuesday	Wednesday	Thursday	Friday	Saturday

Improve Your Skills

Good students develop their skills both inside and outside the classroom. Your *SCORE! Mountain Challenge Workbook* can help. Set aside part of your homework time each day for completing sections from this workbook. Check your progress with the online quizzes as well!

Helping Out at Home

Chores are important. They help us learn how to care for our world!

What chores do you do at home to help?

To help out at home:

- Pick one chore each week to do around your home, like making your bed or setting the table for dinner.

- Then, add a new chore the next week.

- Before you know it, you can look around your home and see what a good job you've done!

Keep track of all your chores by making a chore list or adding them to your weekly schedule!

Try New Things!

Even though you're busy, it's also great to try new things!

Maybe you want to try a new sport, join a new club at school, or read a new book?

Write down something new that you would like to try this week and try to make time to do it!

_____

_____

Make Time for Fun and Relaxation!

Finishing your schoolwork and chores is very important, but you should also make time to spend with your friends and family. Also, don't forget to make time for you!

Your *SCORE! Mountain Challenge Workbook* comes with a fun, interactive online companion. Parents, go online to register your child at **kaptest.com/ scorebooksonline**. Here your child can access 60 exciting math activities and a cool mountain-climbing study partner.

Children, when you log on, you'll be brought to a page where you will find your *SCORE! Mountain Challenge Workbook* cover. You'll also be asked for a **password**, which you will get from a passage in this workbook. So have your workbook handy when you're ready to continue your *SCORE!* Mountain Challenge online, and follow the directions.

Good luck and have fun climbing!

Base Camp

1

Number Sense

Are you ready to begin climbing *SCORE!* Mountain? Let's get started! Good luck!

1. Isabella spent Saturday and Sunday raking leaves. On Saturday, she raked the leaves into **7 large piles**. She raked an **equal number** of piles of leaves on Sunday.

How many piles of leaves did Isabella rake in all? **Write** your answer on the line below.

7

Hint #1:

The word *equal* means **same**. Isabella raked 7 piles of leaves on Saturday and the **same** number of piles on Sunday.

Hint #2:

7 + 7 = ?

Answer: Isabella raked **14 piles** of leaves in all.

7 + 7 = 14

2. Jack's kitten climbed **8 feet** up a tree before stopping to rest. Then the kitten climbed **3 feet** higher.

How many **total feet** did the kitten climb? **Write** your answer on the line below.

_____

Hint #1:

Jack's kitten climbed **8 feet** and then climbed another **3 feet**. You will need to **add** 8 feet and 3 feet.

Hint #2:

8 + 3 = ?

Answer: Jack's kitten climbed a total of **11 feet** up the tree.

8 + 3 = 11

3. Morgan baked **3 batches of cookies** to bring to her friend, Abby.

She used **2 eggs** for the **first batch** of cookies.

She used **4 eggs** for the **second batch** of cookies.

Only **1 egg** was needed for her **third batch** of cookies.

How many **total** eggs did Morgan use to make the three batches of cookies? **Write** your answer on the line below.

_____

Hint #1:
You will need to **add** the number of eggs that Morgan used for **each batch** of cookies to find the **total.**

Hint #2:
2 + 4 + 1 = ?

Answer: Morgan used **7 eggs** to make the three batches of cookies.

2 + 4 + 1 = 7

© Kaplan Publishing, Inc.

4. Miguel gathered seashells at the beach. He placed **7 large**, **white seashells** into his pail. Then he added **6 small**, **brown seashells** to his pail.

How many **total** seashells did Miguel gather? **Write** your answer on the line below.

_____

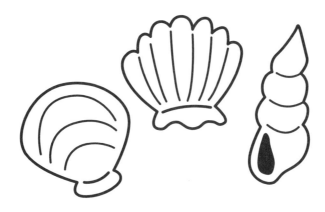

Hint #1:

You need to **add** all of the seashells.

Hint #2:

7 + 6 = ?

Answer: Miguel gathered **13 seashells** in all.

7 + 6 = 13

5. Let's try some more **addition**!

9 + 4 = _____

6 + 3 = _____

5 + 2 = _____

11 + 7 = _____

4 + 1 = _____

Hint:

Add carefully!

Answer: How did you do?

9 + 4 = 13

6 + 3 = 9

5 + 2 = 7

11 + 7 = 18

4 + 1 = 5

Use the chart below to answer questions 6–7.

6. Liam played his favorite game at the carnival.

He needed to score at least **85 points** to win a stuffed teddy bear.

He threw markers at the target below. For each marker that landed on the target, Liam scored either **10 points** or **1 point**.

How many **total** points did Liam score?
Write your answer on the line below.

_____

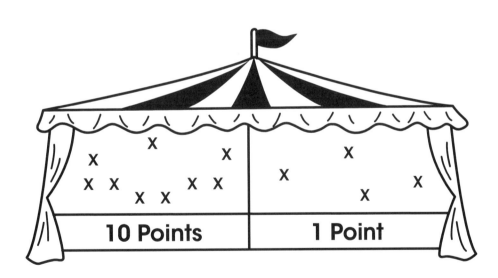

See hints and answer on following page.

Hint #1:

How many **X**s are in the section labeled "**1 Point**"? You can think of this as the **ones place** digit of his total score.

Hint #2:

How many **X**s are in the section labeled "**10 Points**"? Because each **X** here is worth **10 points**, this is the **tens place** digit of his total score.

Answer: Liam scored a total of 94 points on the game at the carnival.

There are **9 X**s in the **10 Point** section. These are worth **90 points**.

There are **4 X**s in the **1 Point** section. These are worth **4 points**.

90 points + 4 points = 94 points

7. Did Liam score enough points to get the stuffed bear? **Write** your answer on the line below.

_____

Hint #1:

Remember, Liam needed **85 points** to get the stuffed bear.

Hint #2:

Remember, Liam scored a total of **94 points**.

Answer: Yes, Liam scored enough points to win the stuffed bear.

94 is **more** than **85**.

94 > 85

8. Today, Jill's Sweet Treats is selling chocolate chip cookies.

The chart below shows how many chocolate chip cookies her first 5 customers ordered.

Cookie Orders	
Customer	**Number of Cookies Ordered**
John	5
Mary	6
Henry	3
Janice	4
Daryl	2

How many **total** chocolate chip cookies did Jill's first 5 customers order? **Write** your answer on the line below.

_____

Hint #1:

Use **addition** to find the total number of cookies ordered.

Hint #2:

5 + 6 + 3 + 4 + 2 = ?

Answer: Jill's first 5 customers ordered a total of **20 chocolate chip cookies**.

5 + 6 + 3 + 4 + 2 = 20

9. Use **subtraction** to solve:

$$15 - 9 = \rule{2cm}{0.4pt}$$

Hint #1:

Subtract 10 from the number **15**. To the difference, **add 1**.

Hint #2:

$$15 - 10 = 5$$
$$5 + 1 = ?$$

Answer: **15 − 9 = 6**

10. Use **addition** to solve:

$$9 + 8 = \underline{\hspace{2cm}}$$

Hint #1:

Add 10 to the number **8**. From the sum, **subtract 1**.

Hint #2:

$10 + 8 = 18$
$18 - 1 = \ ?$

Answer: **9 + 8 = 17**

© Kaplan Publishing, Inc.

12 SCORE! *Mountain Challenge*

11. Help complete the bowling chart below! **Fill in** the blanks.

After each turn, **add** the number of **pins knocked down** to the number of **pins left standing**. The sum is always **10**.

The first one is done for you!

Pins Knocked Down	Pins Left Standing	Addition Fact
3	7	3 + 7 = 10
	5	
4		
	8	
9		

Hint #1:

Use **addition** to finish the chart.

Hint #2:

Pins knocked down + Pins left standing = **10 pins**

Answer: Does your chart look like this?

Pins Knocked Down	Pins Left Standing	Addition Fact
3	7	3 + 7 = 10
5	5	5 + 5 = 10
4	6	4 + 6 = 10
2	8	2 + 8 = 10
9	1	9 + 1 = 10

12. Everyone is excited for the Harvest Day Hayride!

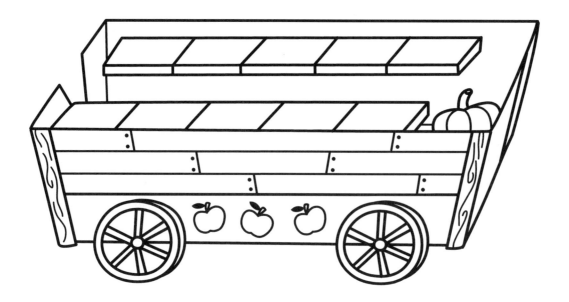

6 students from Mrs. Lane's class are ready to climb aboard.

8 students from Miss Webb's class are waiting in line.

How many **total** students were waiting in line? **Write** your answer below.

_____

Hint #1:

How many students were in each class?

Hint #2:

Use **addition** to find the total number of students waiting in line.

Answer: **14 students** were waiting in line.

6 + 8 = 14

13.

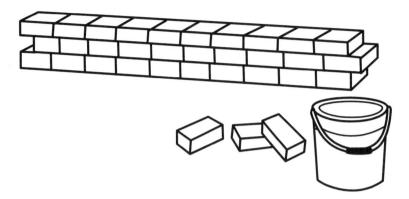

Mr. Jenkins was building a brick wall. He used **10 bricks** for each layer of the wall. He used **80 bricks** total for the wall.

How many layers high was Mr. Jenkins's wall? **Write** your answer on the line below.

_____

Hint #1:

Mr. Jenkins used **10 bricks** for each layer of the wall. To find the total number of layers, **skip count by tens** to **80**.

Hint #2:

You can make a table to find the number of layers.

Number of Bricks	Number of Layers
10 bricks	1 layer
20 bricks	2 layers
30 bricks	3 layers

Continue the table until you reach **80 bricks**.

Answer: Mr. Jenkins built a wall that was **8 layers** high.

Number of Bricks	Number of Layers
10 bricks	1 layer
20 bricks	2 layers
30 bricks	3 layers
40 bricks	4 layers
50 bricks	5 layers
60 bricks	6 layers
70 bricks	7 layers
80 bricks	**8 layers**

14. Emily went to the toy store and saw a dollhouse.

She saw **3 plates** on **each shelf** in the dollhouse. There were **6 shelves total**.

How many **total** plates were there?
Write your answer on the line below.

_____

Hint #1:

Remember, each shelf has **3** plates, and there are **6** shelves in the dollhouse.

Hint #2:

Skip count by **3**s to get the answer.

Answer: Emily counted **18 plates** in the dollhouse.

3, 6, 9, 12, 15, **18**

15. Harry had a collection of **92 baseball cards**.

His card album holds **64 cards**.

How many of Harry's baseball cards do **not** fit into the album? **Write** your answer on the line below.

_____

Hint #1:

Use **subtraction** to solve this problem.

Hint #2:

$$\begin{array}{r} 92 \\ -\ 64 \\ \hline ? \end{array}$$

Answer: 28 of Harry's baseball cards did not fit into his album.

$$\begin{array}{r} 92 \\ -\ 64 \\ \hline 28 \end{array}$$

You're doing a great job so far!
Are you ready for a Challenge Activity?
Good luck!

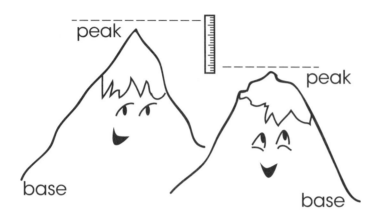

Mount Everest is the highest mountain in the world. It is **29,035 feet high**.

Mount McKinley is **20,320 feet high**. It is the highest mountain in the United States.

a) How many **vertical feet** will you travel if you climb from the **base** of Mount Everest to the **peak** and then back down to the **base** of the mountain? **Write** your answer on the line below.

_____

b) How many feet higher is Mount Everest than Mount McKinley? **Write** your answer on the line below.

_____

c) How many feet are Mount Everest and Mount McKinley **combined**? **Write** your answer on the line below.

_____

Hint #1:

To find the total number of feet, **add** 29,035 and 29,035.

$$\begin{array}{r} 29{,}035 \\ + \ 29{,}035 \\ \hline ? \end{array}$$

You will have to regroup in the **ones column**.
5 + 5 = 10   10 = 1 ten and 0 ones

You will have to regroup when you add the **thousands column**.
9 + 9 = 18   18 = 1 ten thousands and 8 thousands

See hint and answers on following page.

Hint #2:

To find the difference between the height of Mount McKinley and the height of Mount Everest, you will need to **subtract** 20,320 from 29,035.

$$\begin{array}{r} 29,035 \\ -\ 20,320 \\ \hline ? \end{array}$$

You will have to regroup when you subtract in the **hundreds column**.
Change the **9** in the **thousands column** to **8**.
Change the **0** in the **hundreds column** to **10**.

Answers to Challenge Activity:

a) You will travel **58,070 feet** if you climb from the base of Mount Everest to the peak and then back to the base of the mountain.

$$\begin{array}{r} 29,035 \\ +\ 29,035 \\ \hline 58,070 \end{array}$$

b) Mount Everest is **8,715 feet higher** than Mount McKinley.

$$\begin{array}{r} 29,035 \\ -\ 20,320 \\ \hline 8,715 \end{array}$$

c) Mount Everest and Mount McKinley combined are **49,355 feet**.

$$\begin{array}{r} 29,035 \\ +\ 20,320 \\ \hline 49,355 \end{array}$$

© Kaplan Publishing, Inc.

Test

Let's take a quick test and see how much you've learned during this climb up *SCORE!* Mountain. Good luck!

1. Find the sums:

2 + 9 = _____   6 + 6 = _____   7 + 8 = _____

2. Find the differences:

11 − 2 = _____   14 − 7 = _____   17 − 9 = _____

3. Write the number that's represented by the **X**s in the chart below.

Tens	Ones
X X X	X X X
X X	X X X X

Write your answer on the line below.

_____

4. Skip count by **4**s to fill in the blanks below.

4, _____ , 12, 16, _____

5. Write the number that's represented by the **X**s in the chart.

Hundreds	Tens	Ones
X	X X X X X X	X X X X X X X X

Write your answer on the line below.

_____

Answers to test questions:

1. $2 + 9 = $ **11** $6 + 6 = $ **12** $7 + 8 = $ **15**

2. $11 - 2 = $ **9** $14 - 7 = $ **7** $17 - 9 = $ **8**

3. The number is **57**. Add up the amount in each column and then find the total.

Tens	Ones
X X X X X	X X X X X X X

50   +   **7**   = **57**

4. 4, __8__ , 12, 16, __20__

5. The number is **168**. Add up the amount in each column and then find the total.

Hundreds	Tens	Ones
X	X X X X X X	X X X X X X X X

100   +   **60**   +   **8**   = **168**

Celebrate!

Let's take a fun break before we go to the next base camp. You've earned it!

Let's make some fun sock puppets!

What you will need:

- A sock (ask permission from a parent or another adult to use the sock for a puppet)

- A magic marker

- Anything you would like to use to decorate your puppet, such as felt, yarn, and glue

Congratulations! You're on your way up *SCORE!* Mountain.

BASE CAMP **1**

© Kaplan Publishing, Inc.

26

Directions:

- Take your sock and put it over your hand like a glove.

- Push in the area between your thumb and pointer finger to form the puppet's mouth.

- Now it's your chance to be creative!

  - Use your magic marker to give your puppet a face. Choose your favorite colors!

  - You can also use felt and glue to make your puppet's face and give it an outfit!

  - Give your puppet some hair made of yarn!

  - How your puppet looks is up to you!

- Show off your great new puppet to your family and friends!

Good luck and have fun! You deserve it for working so hard!

Base Camp

2

Algebra

Let's continue the climb up *SCORE!* Mountain. Are you ready? Let's get started! Good luck!

SCORE! MOUNTAIN TOP

BASE CAMP 5

BASE CAMP 4

BASE CAMP 3

BASE CAMP 2

BASE CAMP 1

Let's have some fun practicing Algebra!

Let's practice **skip counting**!

1. How many total wings are on **14** birds?
Count by twos to find the total.
Write your answer on the line below.

_____

> **Hint #1:**
>
> Each bird has **2 wings**. Add **2 wings** for each of the **14 birds**.
>
> **2 . . . 4 . . . 6 . . .**

> **Hint #2:**
>
> | Number of Birds | Number of Wings |
> | :---: | :---: |
> | 1 | 2 |
> | 2 | 4 |
> | 3 | 6 |
> | 4 | 8 |

Answer: The 14 birds have **28 wings**.

© Kaplan Publishing, Inc.

2. Students in Mrs. McGinnis's second grade class are collecting empty soda cans. They will receive **five cents** for each can that they collect.

Help the class complete the following chart. **Write** the missing amounts on the lines.

RECYCLING CENTER			
1 can = **5¢**	2 cans = _____ ¢	3 cans = **15¢**	4 cans = _____ ¢
5 cans = _____ ¢	6 cans = **30¢**	7 cans = _____ ¢	8 cans = _____ ¢
9 cans = **45¢**	10 cans = _____ ¢	11 cans = _____ ¢	12 cans = **60¢**
13 cans = _____ ¢	14 cans = _____ ¢	15 cans = _____ ¢	16 cans = _____ ¢
17 cans = **85¢**	18 cans = _____ ¢	19 cans = _____ ¢	20 cans = **$1.00**

Hint #1:

For each can, the class will receive 5¢. Add **5¢** for each can returned.

5 ... 10 ... 15 ...

See hints and answer on following page.

Hint #2:

When you **skip count by 5**, the digit in the ones place will be a **5** or a **0**.

5 . . . _0 . . . _5 . . . _0 . . . _5 . . . _0 . . . _5 . . . _0 . . .

Answer:

 RECYCLING CENTER

1 can = **5¢**	2 cans = **10¢**	3 cans = **15¢**	4 cans = **20¢**
5 cans = **25¢**	6 cans = **30¢**	7 cans = **35¢**	8 cans = **40¢**
9 cans = **45¢**	10 cans = **50¢**	11 cans = **55¢**	12 cans = **60¢**
13 cans = **65¢**	14 cans = **70¢**	15 cans = **75¢**	16 cans = **80¢**
17 cans = **85¢**	18 cans = **90¢**	19 cans = **95¢**	20 cans = **$1.00**

3. Ten numbers have disappeared from the 100 chart below!

Can you help track them down?

Write the missing numbers in the blank squares.

1	2	3	4	5		7	8	9	10
11	12	13	14	15	16	17	18		20
21	22	23		25	26	27	28	29	30
31		33	34	35	36	37	38	39	40
41	42	43	44		46	47	48	49	50
51	52	53	54	55	56	57		59	60
	62	63	64	65	66	67	68	69	70
71	72	73	74	75	76	77	78	79	
81	82	83	84	85	86		88	89	90
91	92		94	95	96	97	98	99	100

Hint #1:

Try counting out loud. Start at **1** and keep counting!

Hint #2:

As you travel **down** each column, the numbers **increase by ten**. As you travel **up** each column, the numbers **decrease by ten**.

Answer: Did you find the missing numbers?

1	2	3	4	5	6	7	8	9	10
11	12	13	14	15	16	17	18	19	20
21	22	23	24	25	26	27	28	29	30
31	32	33	34	35	36	37	38	39	40
41	42	43	44	45	46	47	48	49	50
51	52	53	54	55	56	57	58	59	60
61	62	63	64	65	66	67	68	69	70
71	72	73	74	75	76	77	78	79	80
81	82	83	84	85	86	87	88	89	90
91	92	93	94	95	96	97	98	99	100

© Kaplan Publishing, Inc.

4. There are treasures buried on the 100 chart below!

Read the pieces of maps shown below.

X marks the spots where the treasures may be found. What number belongs where the **X** is? **Write** the missing numbers on the lines below the maps.

Use the 100 chart below to help you.

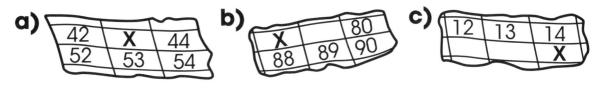

a)

42	X	44
52	53	54

b)

X		80
88	89	90

c)

12	13	14
		X

_____   _____   _____

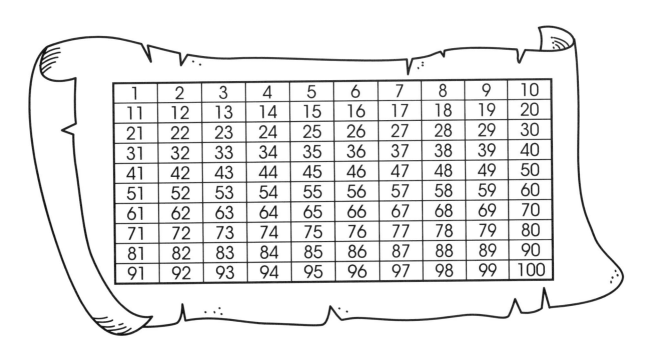

1	2	3	4	5	6	7	8	9	10
11	12	13	14	15	16	17	18	19	20
21	22	23	24	25	26	27	28	29	30
31	32	33	34	35	36	37	38	39	40
41	42	43	44	45	46	47	48	49	50
51	52	53	54	55	56	57	58	59	60
61	62	63	64	65	66	67	68	69	70
71	72	73	74	75	76	77	78	79	80
81	82	83	84	85	86	87	88	89	90
91	92	93	94	95	96	97	98	99	100

See hints and answer on following page.

Hint #1:

Look at the numbers that appear **before**, **after**, **above**, or **below** each **X**.

As you travel **across** each row to the **right**, the numbers **increase by one**.

As you travel **across** each row to the **left**, the numbers **decrease by one**.

Hint #2:

As you travel **down** each column, the numbers **increase by ten**. As you travel **up** each column, the numbers **decrease by ten**.

Answer:

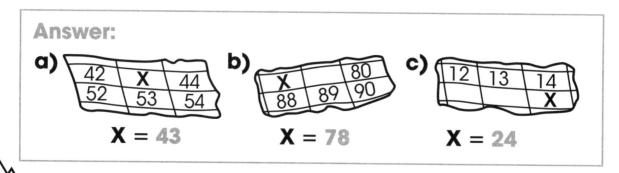

a)

42	X	44
52	53	54

X = 43

b)

X		80
88	89	90

X = 78

c)

12	13	14
		X

X = 24

5. Look at the scales below.

The weight of **2 cylinders** is equal to the weight of **1 cube**.

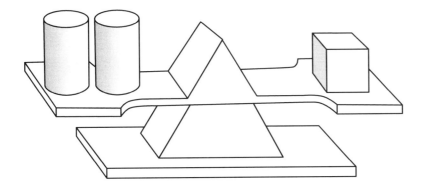

The weight of **3 cubes** is equal to the weight of **1 sphere**.

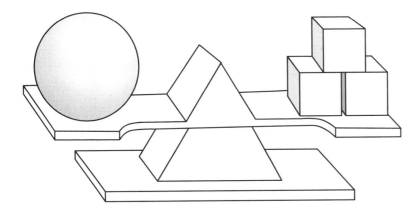

How many **cylinders** are needed to balance **one sphere**? **Write** your answer on the line below.

_____

See hints and answer on following page.

Hint #1:

Because **1 sphere** is equal to **3 cubes**, you will need to find out how many cylinders equal the weight of **3 cubes**.

Hint #2:

1 cube	=	2 cylinders
2 cubes	=	4 cylinders
3 cubes	=	? cylinders

Now do you know how many cylinders are needed to balance 1 sphere?

Answer: **6 cylinders** are needed to balance **1 sphere**.

1 sphere = 3 cubes = **6 cylinders**

6. Look at the math facts below. The hearts ♥ are covering up the **same number**. Identify the number that the hearts are covering. **Write** the number on the line provided.

$$3 + ♥ = 6$$
$$11 - ♥ = 8$$
$$♥ = \underline{\hspace{2cm}}$$

Hint #1:

If the addition fact is $3 + ♥ = 6$, you can change the fact to $6 - 3 = ♥$. Then solve the subtraction fact.

Hint #2:

Make sure each number works for **both the** addition and the subtraction facts!

Answer: Did you find the right number?

$$♥ = 3$$
$$3 + 3 = 6$$
$$11 - 3 = 8$$

© Kaplan Publishing, Inc.

7. Milena created a **repeating pattern** with a deck of playing cards.

If Milena's pattern continues to repeat in the same way, which symbol will appear on the **next** playing card in the pattern? **Write** your answer on the line.

Hint #1:

Look closely at the pattern. Identify where the pattern begins to **repeat**.

Hint #2:

Sometimes it's easier to see a pattern that is written in **letters** rather than **symbols**.

♥ ♣ ♦ ♠

H C D S

Answer:

8. Which animal comes **next** in the pattern below? **Circle** your answer.

 _____

Hint #1:

Look at how the shapes repeat.

Hint #2:

What comes after a **dog** in the pattern?

Answer: The next animal in the pattern is a **cat**.

9. Which object is **missing** from the pattern below? **Circle** your answer.

Hint #1:
Look at how the shapes are repeating.

Hint #2:
What comes after a **book** in the pattern?

Answer: The object missing from the pattern is a **pencil.**

© Kaplan Publishing, Inc.

10. Are the objects below in a pattern?
Circle your answer.

Yes   **No**

Hint #1:

The objects in a **pattern** repeat in the same order. Is this a pattern?

Hint #2:

If it's hard to tell what shape comes next, than it might **not** be a pattern.

Answer: No, this is not a pattern.

The objects **do not** repeat in the same order.

11. Look at the pattern below. What should the **bottom row** look like? **Draw** the missing row.

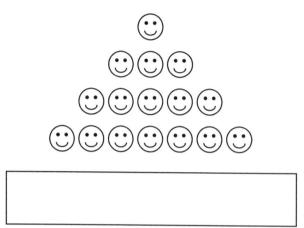

Hint #1:

Count the ☺ in each row. Look for the pattern. How does the pattern grow?

Hint #2:

Does this help you to see the pattern?

Answer: The bottom row will have **9** ☺s.

12. Nancy is building towers with blocks. She is following a **pattern**. How many blocks will she need to build **Tower 4**?

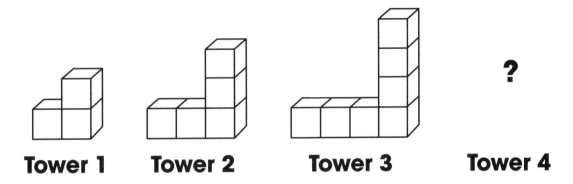

Tower 1   Tower 2   Tower 3   Tower 4

Hint #1:

Count the blocks used in each tower. Do you see a pattern?

Tower 1   **3 blocks**
Tower 2   **5 blocks**
Tower 3   **7 blocks**
Tower 4   **? blocks**

Hint #2:

For each tower, **color** the new blocks that Nancy has added. How many blocks are added each time Nancy builds a new tower?

Answer: Nancy will need a total of **9 blocks** to build tower 4. Here is what it would look like.

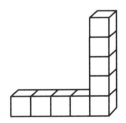

Tower 4

Use the magic number machine below to answer questions 13 and 14.

Miss Lane's second grade class has a **magic number machine** in their classroom.

When a card is placed in the slot marked **IN**, the machine will **add 5** to the number and then **subtract 3**.

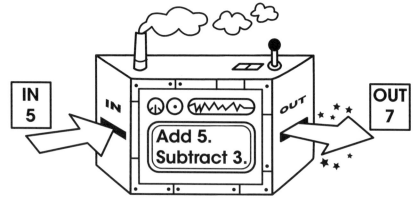

IN
5

OUT
7

13. If

IN
6

is fed into the machine, **circle** the card that would come out.

| **OUT** | **OUT** | **OUT** | **OUT** |
| **6** | **7** | **8** | **9** |

Hint #1:

Remember, the magic number machine **adds 5** to the number, then **subtracts 3** from the sum.

Hint #2:

What is **6 + 5**? Take that sum and **subtract 3**.

© Kaplan Publishing, Inc.

Answer:

OUT
8
would come out.

6 + 5 = 11

11 − 3 = **8**

14. Let's try another one!

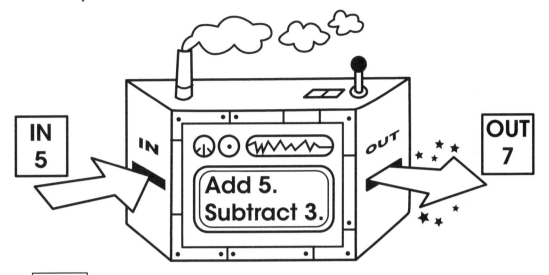

If | **IN** **12** | is fed into the machine, **circle** the card that would come out.

| **OUT** **13** | | **OUT** **14** | | **OUT** **15** | | **OUT** **16** |

Hint #1:

Remember, the magic number machine **adds 5** to the number, then **subtracts 3** from the sum.

Hint #2:

What is **12 + 5**? Take that sum and **subtract 3**.

Answer:

| **OUT** **14** | would come out.

12 + 5 = 17

17 − 3 = **14**

15. Look at the function table below. One number goes **in** and another comes **out**. Use the **rule** to fill in the missing numbers.

Rule: Add 6				
IN	2	5	1	4
OUT	8	11		

Hint #1:

First, read the rule. Then, read the number next to the word **IN**.

Hint #2:

Add **carefully**!

Answer:

Rule: Add 6				
IN	2	5	1	4
OUT	8	11	7	10

$1 + 6 = \mathbf{7}$

$4 + 6 = \mathbf{10}$

© Kaplan Publishing, Inc.

**You are doing a great job so far!
Are you ready for a Challenge Activity?
Good luck!**

Let's find out some interesting facts about
U.S. presidents!

Read each question. Use the number above each
letter in the chart to find the answer. **Write** that number
on the line below.

0	1	2	3	4	5	6	7	8	9
B	C	D	F	G	H	J	K	L	M

a) How many U.S. presidents were born
in Virginia?

Coded Answer: J + D =

Answer: _____

b) How many U.S. presidents were less than 6 feet tall?

Coded Answer: L + L + K =   **Answer:** _____

c) How many U.S. presidents have had the first name *James*?

Coded Answer: (G + F) − C =   **Answer:** _____

Hint #1:	Hint #2:
Replace the letters with numbers from the code chart and solve! **Example:** H + K = ? 　　　　　**5 + 7 = 12**	Solve the fact **inside the parentheses** first. **Example:** D + (L − G) = ? 　　　　2 + (8 − 4) = 　　　　**2 + 4 = 6**

Answers to Challenge Activity:

a) How many U.S presidents were born in Virginia?　8
6 + 2 = **8**

b) How many U.S. presidents were less than 6 feet tall?　23
8 + 8 + 7 = **23**

c) How many U.S. presidents have had the first name *James*?　6
(4 + 3) − 1 = **6**

© Kaplan Publishing, Inc.

Test

Let's take a quick test and see how much you've learned during this climb up **SCORE!** Mountain. Good luck!

1. Skip count by 3s and fill in the blanks.

3, _____ , **9**, _____ , _____ , **18**,

_____ , _____ , _____ , **30**

2. Fill in the missing numbers on the 100 chart.

1	2	3	4	5	6	7	8	9	10
11	12		14	15	16	17	18	19	20
21	22	23		25	26	27	28	29	30
31	32	33	34	35		37	38	39	40
41	42	43	44	45	46	47	48	49	50
51	52	53	54	55	56		58	59	60
	62	63	64	65	66	67	68	69	
71		73	74	75	76	77	78	79	80
81	82	83	84		86	87	88	89	90
91	92	93	94	95	96			99	100

3. Fill in the missing shapes in the repeating pattern below.

4. Look at the growing pattern. Draw the 3rd figure.

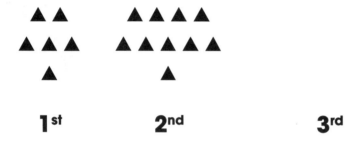

1st   2nd   3rd

5. Complete the rule table below.

Rule: Add 8				
IN	5	2	8	6
OUT				

Answers to test questions:

1. 3, **6**, 9, **12**, **15**, 18, **21**, **24**, **27**, 30

2. Were you able to finish the chart?

1	2	3	4	5	6	7	8	9	10
11	12	**13**	14	15	16	17	18	19	20
21	22	23	**24**	25	26	27	28	29	30
31	32	33	34	35	**36**	37	38	39	40
41	42	43	44	45	46	47	48	49	50
51	52	53	54	55	56	**57**	58	59	60
61	62	63	64	65	66	67	68	69	**70**
71	**72**	73	74	75	76	77	78	79	80
81	82	83	84	**85**	86	87	88	89	90
91	92	93	94	95	96	**97**	**98**	99	100

3. Were you able to finish the pattern?

▲ ▼ ■ ● ✤ ▲ ▼ ■ ● ✤ ▲ ▼ ■ ● ✤ ▲

4. The top row of the pattern is **increasing by 2 ▲s.**
The middle row of the pattern is **increasing by 2 ▲s.**
The bottom row of the pattern is **staying the same.**

▲ ▲	▲ ▲ ▲ ▲	▲ ▲ ▲ ▲ ▲ ▲
▲ ▲ ▲	▲ ▲ ▲ ▲ ▲	▲ ▲ ▲ ▲ ▲ ▲ ▲
▲	▲	▲
1st	**2nd**	**3rd**

5.

Rule: Add 8				
IN	5	2	8	6
OUT	13	10	16	14

Celebrate!

Let's take a fun break before we go to the next base camp. You've earned it!

Here's a fun science trick you can share with your family and friends!

What you will need:

- A raisin

- A glass of clear soda water

Congratulations! You're getting closer to the top of *SCORE!* Mountain.

Directions:

- This is a fun and simple science trick! Fill a clear glass with soda water and drop in your raisin.

- The wrinkly surface of the raisin will trap air bubbles from the soda water, causing it to rise from the bottom of the glass to the surface.

- When enough bubbles surrounding your floating raisin break free, the raisin will sink back down again.

- The raisin will continue to rise and fall in your glass—it's science magic!

- This science trick works best if your soda water is extra bubbly.

- Show off this science trick to your family and friends!

- Have fun pretending that you are in control of the "floating raisin" and that you are commanding it to rise and fall in the glass!

Good luck and have fun! You deserve it for working so hard!

Base Camp

3

Geometry

Are you ready for another fun climb up *SCORE!* Mountain? Let's get started! Good luck!

SCORE! MOUNTAIN TOP

BASE CAMP 5

BASE CAMP 4

BASE CAMP 3

BASE CAMP 2

BASE CAMP 1

Let's learn about some **shapes**!

1. Read the description of the object.
Is it a **cube** or is it a **sphere**?
Write your answer on the line.

cube   sphere

It has six faces. That's quite clear.
Is it a cube, or is it a sphere?   _____

Hint #1:

Cubes have **faces**, which are flat sides.

Hint #2:

A ball rolls easily. A ball is a **sphere**.

© Kaplan Publishing, Inc.

Answer: cube

2. Let's try again! Is it a **cube** or is it a **sphere**? **Write** your answer on the line.

cube

sphere

A ball has no edges
and rolls far and near.
Is it a cube? Is it a sphere?

_____

Hint:

Remember the difference between a cube and a sphere!

Answer: sphere

3. Which shape is it? **Circle** your answer.

This shape has **no sides** or **corners**.

A. circle

B. square

C. triangle

D. rectangle

Hint #1:
Which shape looks like a CD or a cookie?

Hint #2:
Which shape has **no sides** or **corners**?

Answer: Choice **A** is correct.

A has **no** sides or corners. A CD and some cookies are **circles**.

circle

4. Which shape is it? **Circle** your answer.

This shape has **4 equal sides** and **4 corners**.

A. ◯
circle

B. ☐
square

C. △
triangle

D. ▭
rectangle

Hint #1:

Count the number of **sides** and **corners** for each shape.

Hint #2:

Which shape has **4 equal sides** and **4 corners**?

Answer: Choice **B** is correct.

A ☐ has **4 equal sides** and **4 corners**.

square

5. **Let's try again!** Which shape is it?
Circle your answer.

This shape usually has **2 short sides**
and **2 long sides**.

A.
circle

B. ☐
square

C. △
triangle

D. ▭
rectangle

Hint #1:
Count the **long** and
short sides of each
shape.

Hint #2:
Which shape has
2 short sides and
2 long sides?

Answer: Choice **D** is correct.

A ▭ has **2 short sides** and **2 long sides**.
rectangle

6. One more time! Which shape is it? Circle your answer.

This shape has **3 sides** and **3 corners**.

A.
circle

B.
square

C. △
triangle

D. ▭
rectangle

Hint #1:
Which shape looks like a slice of pizza?

Hint #2:
Which shape has **3 sides** and **3 corners**?

Answer: Choice **C** is correct.

A △ has **3 sides** and **3 corners**.

triangle

7. Look at the heart below. Is it **symmetrical**?

If it is **symmetrical, color** it **yellow**.
If it is **not symmetrical, color** it **blue**.

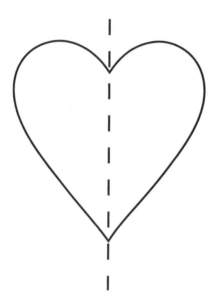

Hint #1:

If you folded the heart on the dotted line, would both halves match up **exactly**? If they would, then it is **symmetrical**.

Hint #2:

If you folded the heart on the dotted line and both halves did **not** match up exactly, then it would **not** be **symmetrical**.

Answer: The heart is **symmetrical**. Both halves match when folded.
Did you color it **yellow**?

8. Look at the apple below. Is it **symmetrical**?

If it is **symmetrical**, **color** it **green**.
If it is **not symmetrical**, **color** it **red**.

Hint #1:

If you folded the apple on the dotted line, would both halves match up exactly? If they would, then it is **symmetrical**.

Hint #2:

If you folded the apple on the dotted line and both halves did **not** match up exactly, then it is **not symmetrical**.

Answer: The apple is not symmetrical. The halves do not match when folded.
Did you color it **red**?

9. Let's try again! Look at the butterfly below.
Is it **symmetrical**?

If it is **symmetrical, color** it **purple**.
If it is **not symmetrical, color** it **yellow.**

Hint #1:

If you folded the butterfly on the dotted line, would both halves match up exactly? If they would, then it is **symmetrical**.

Hint #2:

If you folded the butterfly on the dotted line and both halves did **not** match up exactly, then it would **not** be **symmetrical**.

Answer: The butterfly is **symmetrical**.
The halves match.
Did you color it **purple**?

© Kaplan Publishing, Inc.

10. **One more time!** Look at the house below.
Is it **symmetrical**?

If it is **symmetrical**, **color** it **pink**.
If it is **not symmetrical**, **color** it **blue**.

Hint #1:
If you folded the house on the dotted line, would both halves match up exactly? If they would, then it is **symmetrical**.

Hint #2:
If you folded the house on the dotted line and both halves did **not** match up exactly, then it would **not** be **symmetrical**.

Answer: The house is not symmetrical. The halves do not match.
Did you color it **blue**?

11. Point the arrow in the right direction!

Read the directions in **Box A** and **Box B**, and **draw** the missing arrow in **Box C**.

A. Here is an arrow.	**B. Turn** This is what the arrow from **Box A** will look like if it is **turned** once clockwise.	**C.** **Draw** what the arrow from **Box B** will look like if it is **turned** once clockwise.

Hint #1:

Clockwise means in the same direction that the hands of a clock move. If an arrow pointing to the **right** is turned once **clockwise**, the arrow will be pointing **down**.

Hint #2:

If an arrow that is pointing **down** is turned once **clockwise**, it will be pointing to the **left**.

© Kaplan Publishing, Inc.

Answer: Did you draw your arrow in the correct direction?

A.	B. Turn	C.
Here is an arrow.	This is what the arrow from **Box A** will look like if it is **turned** once clockwise.	**Draw** what the arrow from **Box B** will look like if it is **turned** once clockwise.

12. Let's measure!

Measure the following body parts using an **inch ruler**. **Write** your measurements in the chart below.

If you don't have a ruler, use the ruler below.

Body Part	Measurement (Inches)
the **length** of your nose	
the **width** of your palm	
the **width** of your smile	
the **length** of your thumb	

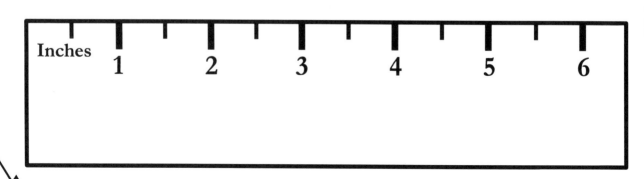

© Kaplan Publishing, Inc.

Hint #1:

Be sure that the **beginning** of your ruler is placed at the **start** of the body part that you are measuring.

Hint #2:

Measure carefully!

Answer: Everyone's measurements will be **different**, because every person is **different**!

13. Let's measure some flower stems!

Measure the height of each flower below using a **centimeter ruler**.

Write the measurements at the **top** of each flower. Label the measurements "**cm**."

If you don't have a centimeter ruler, use the ruler below.

Flower A   Flower B   Flower C

| 1 | 2 | 3 | 4 | 5 | 6 | 7 | 8 | 9 | 10 | 11 | 12 | 13 | 14 | 15 |

Centimeters

Hint #1:

Place the centimeter ruler **vertically** beside the first flower. Be sure that the **beginning** of the ruler is matched up with the **start** of the flower.

Hint #2:

Place your finger at the **top** of each flower. What number on the centimeter ruler lines up with the top of the flower?

Answer: How did you do?

Flower A: 6 cm
Flower B: 9 cm
Flower C: 12 cm

14. Is it **more** than a pound or **less** than a pound?

Circle your answer.

pencil

more than a pound   less than a pound

Hint #1:

If it weighs **more** than a loaf of bread, it probably weighs **more** than one pound.

Hint #2:

If it weighs **less** than a loaf of bread, it probably weighs **less** than one pound.

Answer:

A **pencil** weighs **less than a pound**.

15. On each line, **circle** the **greater** amount of lemonade.

Look at the chart on the next page for help.

1 cup = 8 fluid ounces
1 pint = 2 cups

a) 1 cup **or** 5 ounces

b) 2 cups **or** 3 pints

c) 1 pint **or** 1 cup

25¢

See hint and answers on following page.

© Kaplan Publishing, Inc.

Hint:

Look at the chart below for help.

Ounces	Cup(s)	Pint(s)
8	1	
16	2	1
24	3	
32	4	2
40	5	
48	6	3

Answer:

a)   (1 cup)   **or**   5 ounces

b)   2 cups   **or**   (3 pints)

c)   (1 pint)   **or**   1 cup

Challenge Activity

You're doing a great job so far! Are you ready for a Challenge Activity? Good luck!

a) **Circle** and **color** the letters that are **symmetrical**.

b) Try again! **Circle** and **color** the letters that are **symmetrical**.

 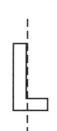  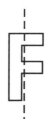 

c) One more time! **Circle** and **color** the letters that are **symmetrical**.

 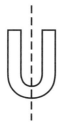   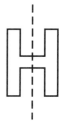

See hints and answers on following page.

Hint #1:

If you folded the letter on the dotted line, would both halves match up exactly? If they would, then it is **symmetrical**.

Hint #2:

If you folded the letter on the dotted line and both halves did **not** match up exactly, then it would **not be symmetrical**.

Answers to Challenge Activity:

a) A R O N Z

b) T L P F Q

c) M U V W H

Let's take a quick test and see how much you've learned during this climb up *SCORE!* Mountain. Good luck!

1. Draw a cube below.

2. Give this triangle a line of symmetry.

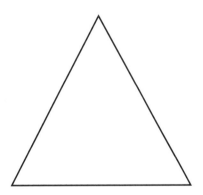

3. Circle your answer.

The weight of a horse is:

less than one pound   more than one pound

4. Circle your answer.

The length of a dollar bill is:

less than one inch   more than one inch

5. Circle the greatest capacity.

16 ounces   4 cups   3 pints

Answers to test questions:

1.

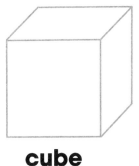

cube

2.

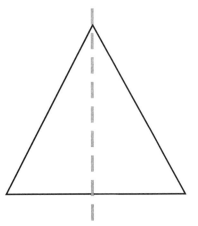

3. The weight of a horse is **more than one pound**.

4. The length of a dollar bill is **more than one inch**.

5. Circle the greatest capacity.

16 ounces   4 cups   3 pints

Celebrate!

Let's take a fun break before we go to the next base camp. You've earned it!

Let's design a flag!

Ask an adult to help you cut out the flag pattern. Design a special flag for your favorite team or group!

Be creative! How your flag looks is up to you!

Congratulations! You're halfway up to the top of *SCORE!* Mountain.

BASE CAMP 1

BASE CAMP 2

BASE CAMP 3

Good luck and have fun! You deserve it for working so hard!

Base Camp

4

Probability and Statistics

Wow! you're getting close to the top of *SCORE!* Mountain. Are you ready for another fun climb? Let's get started! Good luck!

SCORE! MOUNTAIN TOP

BASE CAMP 5

BASE CAMP 4

BASE CAMP 3

BASE CAMP 2

BASE CAMP 1

1. What is **certain**? What is **impossible**?
Circle your answer.

A dog will sing like a person.

impossible   certain

Hint #1:

Remember, if an event will definitely happen, it is **certain**.

Hint #2:

Remember, if an event will never happen, it is **impossible**.

Answer:

It is impossible that a dog will sing like a person.

2. Let's try again!

Is it **certain** or **impossible**?
Circle your answer.

A baby will read a book.

impossible   certain

Hint #1:

Remember, if an event
will definitely happen, it
is **certain**.

Hint #2:

Remember, if an event
will never happen, it is
impossible.

Answer:

It is **impossible** that a baby will read a book.

3. Read the event below and decide if
it is **likely** or **unlikely** to happen.
Circle your answer.

I will have a test in school every day.

likely   unlikely

Hint #1:
Remember, **likely** events
have a good chance of
happening.

Hint #2:
Unlikely events
have little chance of
happening.

Answer: Everyone's answers will be **different**, because
everyone's life is **different**!

It is unlikely that I will have a test in school every day.

4. Let's try again!

Read the event below. Is it **likely** or **unlikely** to happen? **Circle** your answer.

There will be a penguin in your classroom today.

likely   unlikely

Hint #1:
Remember, **likely** events have a good chance of happening.

Hint #2:
Unlikely events have little chance of happening.

Answer:
It is unlikely that there will be a penguin in your classroom today.

5. Some events are **more likely**, while other events are **less likely**.

Look at the pair of events.

Circle the event that is **more likely** to happen.

The moon will come out in the morning.

OR

The moon will come out at night.

Hint #1:
Circle the event that has a **greater** chance of happening.

Hint #2:
Imagine each event. Is the event **likely** or **unlikely**?

Answer:
The moon will come out in the morning

OR

The moon will come out at night.

6. Which is **less likely**?

Look at the pair of events.

Circle the event that is **less likely** to happen.

You will eat a sandwich.

OR

You will eat a book.

Hint #1:

Read each event carefully!

Hint #2:

Imagine each event. Is the event **likely** or **unlikely**?

Answer:

You will eat a sandwich.

OR

(You will eat a book.)

7. Let's conduct an **experiment**!

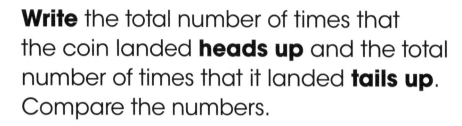

Flip a penny **20 times**. After each flip, **color** in the box on the chart on the next page to show how the penny landed.

Write the total number of times that the coin landed **heads up** and the total number of times that it landed **tails up**. Compare the numbers.

Hint #1:

At the end of **10 flips**, the **most likely** outcome is that your penny will have landed heads up **5 times** and tails up **5 times**. How do your results compare?

Hint #2:

At the end of **20 flips**, the **most likely** outcome is that your penny will have landed heads up **10 times** and tails up **10 times**. How do your results compare?

© Kaplan Publishing, Inc.

Flip Number	Heads Up	Tails Up
Flip 1		
Flip 2		
Flip 3		
Flip 4		
Flip 5		
Flip 6		
Flip 7		
Flip 8		
Flip 9		
Flip 10		
Flip 11		
Flip 12		
Flip 13		
Flip 14		
Flip 15		
Flip 16		
Flip 17		
Flip 18		
Flip 19		
Flip 20		
TOTAL		

Answer: Everyone's results will be different.

Were you surprised by your results?

8. Let's conduct a probability experiment using **2 pennies**!

Flip the 2 pennies **10 times**.

After each flip, place an **X** in the column next to the outcome in the chart on the next page.

When you're done, find the **total** number of **X**s for each outcome. Compare the numbers.

Double Coin Flip

Outcomes	Flip Number										TOTAL
	1	2	3	4	5	6	7	8	9	10	
1 coin heads up, 1 coin tails up											
Both coins heads up											
Both coins tails up											

Hint #1:

Write the results of each flip in the right box!

Hint #2:

Flip carefully!

Answer: Everyone's results will be different.
Were you surprised by your results?

9. A **number cube** contains each of the six numbers shown below.

1	2	3	4	5	6

Which of the following is **more likely** to be rolled? **Circle** your answer choice.

a number greater than 2

        OR

an even number

Hint #1:

The option with the **most** outcomes has the **best chance** of being rolled.

Hint #2:

Here's an example:

a number greater than 5   **OR**   a number less than 4
1 outcome: 6   **3 outcomes: 1, 2, 3**

A number less than 4 is **more likely** to be rolled than a number greater than 5.

Answer:

A number greater than 2 (3, 4, 5, 6) is more likely to be rolled than **an even number** (2, 4, 6).

10. Laurie wrote the name of **each day** on a slip of paper and placed the slips in a bowl.

What is the chance that Laurie will reach into the bag and pull out the name of a day that has **6** letters?

_____ out of _____

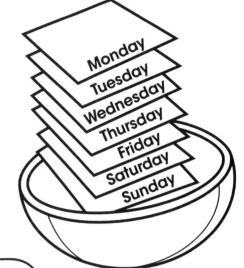

Hint #1:

There is only **1 day** of the week that has a name that begins with **W**.

There are **6 days** with names that do **not** begin with **F**.

There are **7 days** of the week in all.

Hint #2:

The chance of Laurie reaching into the bag and pulling out the name of a day that begins with **S** is **2 out of 7**. There are **2 days** with names that begin with the letter **S** and **7 days** of the week in all.

Answer:

3 out of 7

11. Tom will win a trophy if he spins an **even number** on the spinner below. How likely is Tom to win the prize? **Circle** your answer.

certain   likely   unlikely   impossible

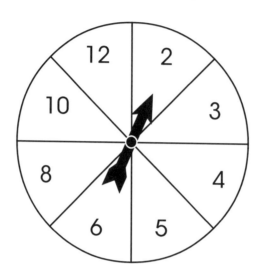

Hint #1:

Even numbers: 2, 4, 6, 8, 10, 12
Odd numbers: 3, 5

Hint #2:

There are **more** even numbers than odd numbers.

Answer:

It is **likely** that Tom will win a trophy.

12. Now it's Sally's turn to spin the spinner!

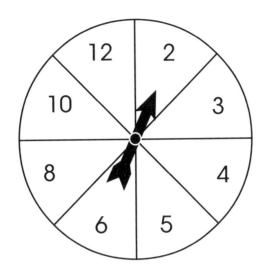

Sally will win a doll if she spins a **number greater than 1**. How likely is Sally to win the prize? **Circle** your answer.

certain   likely   unlikely   impossible

Hint #1:
Remember, if an event will definitely happen, it is **certain**.

Hint #2:
If an event will never happen, it is **impossible**.

Answer:
It is certain that Sally will win a doll. **All** the numbers on the spinner are greater than 1.

13. **Doug has** a bag with **9 red marbles**, **7 blue marbles**, and **1 green marble**. If he picked **1 marble** from the bag without looking, how would you describe his chances of drawing a **green marble**? **Circle** your answer.

certain   likely   unlikely   impossible

Hint #1:

Because there are **17 marbles** in the bag and only **1 marble** is **green**, the chance of drawing a green marble is **low**.

Hint #2:

Doug has a **1 in 17** chance of drawing a green marble.

Answer: It is **unlikely** that Doug will draw a green marble.

14. Cindy has a box with **24 chocolate chip cookies**, **6 sugar cookies**, and **3 peanut butter cookies**.

If she took one without looking, how would you describe her chances of getting a **chocolate chip cookie**? **Circle** your answer.

certain   likely   unlikely   impossible

Hint #1:
There are a total of **33 cookies** in the box.

Hint #2:
Most of the cookies are chocolate chip cookies.

Answer: It is **likely** that she will get a chocolate chip cookie.

15. José put the number cards below on a table.

| 19 | 6 | 8 | 18 | 11 |

| 14 | 17 | 4 | 12 | 2 |

If Jose picked one card without looking, how would you describe his chances of getting a **1-digit**, **odd number**? **Circle** your answer.

certain   likely   unlikely   impossible

Hint #1:
There are **10** possible cards that José can choose.

Hint #2:
How many cards have a 1-digit, odd number?

Answer: It is **impossible** for José to pick a card with a 1-digit odd number on it.

None of the cards has a 1-digit odd number!

Challenge Activity

You're doing a great job so far!
Are you ready for a Challenge Activity?
Good luck!

Today is **sandwich day** at Big Al's Deli!

Customers can choose from:

- **3** breads: **wheat**, **white**, and **rye**
- **2** meats: **ham** and **turkey**
- **3** cheeses: **Swiss**, **American**, and **cheddar**

Big Al claims that he can create **18 different sandwiches** using the different breads, meats, and cheeses listed on his sign.

How many of these sandwiches can you identify? **Write** the sandwiches in the box below. The first sandwich has been made for you!

Sandwich Number	Bread	Meat	Cheese
1	Wheat	Ham	Swiss
2			
3			
4			
5			
6			
7			
8			
9			
10			
11			
12			
13			
14			
15			
16			
17			
18			

Remember, each sandwich must include: **1** type of bread, **1** type of meat, and **1** type of cheese.

Make a list of the different sandwiches that you identify.

Answer: Did you figure out all 18 sandwiches?

Sandwich Number	Bread	Meat	Cheese
1	Wheat	Ham	Swiss
2	Wheat	Ham	American
3	Wheat	Ham	Cheddar
4	Wheat	Turkey	Swiss
5	Wheat	Turkey	American
6	Wheat	Turkey	Cheddar
7	White	Ham	Swiss
8	White	Ham	American
9	White	Ham	Cheddar
10	White	Turkey	Swiss
11	White	Turkey	American
12	White	Turkey	Cheddar
13	Rye	Ham	Swiss
14	Rye	Ham	American
15	Rye	Ham	Cheddar
16	Rye	Turkey	Swiss
17	Rye	Turkey	American
18	Rye	Turkey	Cheddar

Let's take a quick test and see how much you've learned during this climb up *SCORE!* Mountain. Good luck!

1. Put a **C** next to the event if it is **certain** to happen. Put an **I** next to the event if it is **impossible**.

   A horse will dance and talk. _____

2. Put an **L** next to the event if it is **likely** to happen. Put a **U** next to the event if it is **unlikely** to happen.

   You will fly in a helicopter. _____

3. Ten balls are in a bag: **1 white**, **3 red**, and **6 black**. If you reach into the bag and take a ball without looking, what color ball are you **most likely** to pick?

a _____ ball

4. Look at the carnival spinner.

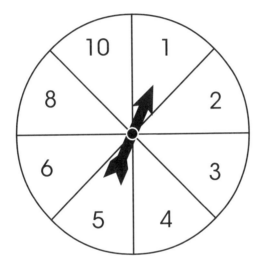

What are the chances that you will spin a number less than 7? **Circle** your answer.

likely   unlikely

5. Sue Ellen is going on vacation.

She has **2 skirts**: a **red** skirt and a **blue** skirt.

She has **2 shirts**: a **white** shirt and a **yellow** shirt.

List the 4 different outfits that Sue Ellen can wear in the chart below.

Outfit 1:	Outfit 2:	Outfit 3:	Outfit 4:
shirt:	shirt:	shirt:	shirt:
skirt:	skirt:	skirt:	skirt:

Answers to test questions:

1. I

It is **impossible** that a horse will dance and talk.

2. U

It is **unlikely** that you will fly in a helicopter.

3. You are **most likely** to pick a black **ball**.
There are **more** black balls than any other color.

4. You are likely to spin a number less than 7.

5. The order of the outfits in your list may be different from the order in the table below.

Outfit 1:	Outfit 2:	Outfit 3:	Outfit 4:
shirt: yellow	shirt: white	shirt: yellow	shirt: white
skirt: red	skirt: red	skirt: blue	skirt: blue

Celebrate!

Let's take a fun break before we go to the next base camp. You've earned it!

Let's play Search for a Star!

You will need:

- A friend or family member to play with
- 12 small slips of paper (all the same size)

Congratulations! You're getting closer to the top of *SCORE!* Mountain.

- A piece of paper for each player
- A pencil for each player
- A small paper bag

Directions:

- Write each letter in the word **STAR** on a slip of paper.

- Fold each slip once.

- Place the slips in the paper bag.

- Repeat this **3 times**. When you are done, there will be **3** of each letter in the word **STAR** in the bag.

- Each player takes a turn reaching into the bag and picking a slip of paper.

- The player reads the letter. Then on the sheet of paper, the player writes the letter.

- The player folds the slip and returns it to the bag.

- The first player to pull out each of the letters **S**, **T**, **A**, and **R** and who can spell the word **STAR** is the winner!

Continued on next page.

- The letters do not have to be pulled out in order.

- How many turns will it take you to spell the word **STAR**?

Good luck and have fun! You deserve it for working so hard!

Base Camp

5

You are really getting close to the top of *SCORE!* Mountain. Great work! Let's keep going! Good luck!

Interpreting Data

BASE CAMP 1

BASE CAMP 2

BASE CAMP 3

BASE CAMP 4

BASE CAMP 5

SCORE! MOUNTAIN TOP

1. Look at the tally chart below.

Favorite Season	
Season	**Tally**
Winter	~~IIII~~ ~~IIII~~ III
Spring	~~IIII~~ III
Summer	~~IIII~~ IIII
Fall	~~IIII~~ ~~IIII~~ II

Which season did the **greatest** number of students choose as their favorite? **Circle** your answer.

Winter   Spring   Summer   Fall

Hint #1:

Count the **tally marks**! Each tally mark stands for **1 student**.

Each ꧂ stands for **5 students**.

Hint #2:

The season that the **greatest** number of students chose will have the **most** number of tally marks.

Answer: Winter was chosen by the greatest number of students.

13 students chose winter as their favorite season.

2. Let's look at the tally chart again!

Favorite Season	
Season	**Tally**
Winter	⑅ ⑅ III
Spring	⑅ III
Summer	⑅ IIII
Fall	⑅ ⑅ II

Which season did the **least** number of students choose as their favorite? **Circle** your answer.

Winter   Spring   Summer   Fall

Hint #1:

Count the tally marks! Each tally mark stands for **1 student**.

Each ⑅ stands for

5 students.

Hint #2:

The season that the **least** number of students chose will have the **least** number of tally marks.

Answer: **Spring** was chosen by the **least** number of students. Only **8 students** chose spring as their favorite season.

© Kaplan Publishing, Inc.

3. Fruit not only tastes delicious, it's good for you too!

The chart lists **6 fruits** and the **number of calories** in each.

Fruit	Calories
Orange	60 calories
Peach	40 calories
Apple	80 calories
Tangerine	35 calories
Banana	105 calories
Mango	135 calories

Which fruit has the **greater number** of calories? **Circle** the correct answer.

a)

an apple   **OR**   an orange

See hints and answer on following page.

b)

a mango   **OR**   a peach

c)

a tangerine   **OR**   a banana

Hint #1:

Read and **compare** the numbers next to each fruit.

Hint #2:

Look closely at the numbers next to each fruit. Pick the fruits that have the **greatest number**.

Answer:

a) An **apple** has **more calories** than an orange. An apple has **80 calories**. An orange has **60 calories**.

b) A **mango** has **more calories** than a peach. A mango has **135 calories**. A peach has **40 calories**.

c) A **banana** has **more calories** than a tangerine. A banana has **105 calories**. A tangerine has **35 calories**.

4. Let's look at the fruit chart again!

Fruit	Calories
Orange	60 calories
Peach	40 calories
Apple	80 calories
Tangerine	35 calories
Banana	105 calories
Mango	135 calories

a) Which fruit has the **greatest** number of calories? _____

b) Which fruit has the **least** number of calories? _____

See hints and answer on following page.

Hint #1:

The **biggest number** is next to the fruit with the **greatest number of calories**.

Hint #2:

The **smallest number** is next to the fruit with the **least number of calories**.

Answer:

a) Mangoes have the **greatest** number of calories. Mangoes have 135 calories.

b) Tangerines have the **least** number of calories. Tangerines have 35 calories.

5. David made a list of each of his friends' favorite flavors of ice cream.

Here is David's list.

Favorite Flavors of Ice Cream			
Chocolate	Vanilla	Vanilla	Vanilla
Vanilla	Peppermint	Chocolate	Strawberry
Strawberry	Vanilla	Strawberry	Chocolate
Vanilla	Chocolate	Peppermint	Vanilla

Let's make a **tally chart** to show the information on David's list!

Fill in the tally marks in the chart below.

Favorite Flavor of Ice Cream	Tally
Strawberry	
Chocolate	
Vanilla	
Peppermint	

See hints and answer on following page.

Hint #1:

Make each **tally mark** (**I**) worth one ice cream choice.

Hint #2:

Count carefully and make sure you put the right tally next to the right type of ice cream.

Answer: Your tally chart should look like this.

Favorite Flavor of Ice Cream	Tally
Strawberry	III
Chocolate	IIII
Vanilla	卌 II
Peppermint	II

6. Look back at your **Favorite Flavor of Ice Cream** tally chart from question 5.

Which flavor of ice cream did the **greatest** number of students choose? **Circle** your answer.

Chocolate   Strawberry   Peppermint   Vanilla

Hint #1:

Count up your tally marks! Each tally mark

stands for **1 student**.
Each 𝍷𝍷 stands for

5 students.

Hint #2:

The ice cream flavor that the **greatest** number of students chose will have the **most** number of tally marks.

Answer:

Vanilla was chosen by the greatest number of students. **7 students** chose vanilla.

7. The chart below shows the number of **gold**, **silver**, and **bronze** medals won by **Germany**, the **United States**, **Canada**, **Austria**, and **Russia** at the 2006 Olympics.

Medals Won at the 2006 Olympics				
Country	Number Of Medals Won			
	Gold	Silver	Bronze	Total
Germany	11	12	6	29
United States	9	9	7	25
Canada	7	10	7	24
Austria	9	7	7	23
Russia	8	6	8	22

Which country earned the **most** gold medals?

_____

Hint #1:

Place your finger on the name of a country. Drag your finger to the right. Read the number of **gold**, **silver**, and **bronze** medals earned by that country.

Hint #2:

The country with the **greatest number** under each type of medal won the **most**.

Answer: Germany earned the most gold medals. Germany earned **11** gold medals.

8. Let's look at the **Medals Won at the 2006 Olympics** chart one more time!

Medals Won at the 2006 Olympics				
Country	**Number of Medals Won**			
	Gold	**Silver**	**Bronze**	**Total**
Germany	11	12	6	29
United States	9	9	7	25
Canada	7	10	7	24
Austria	9	7	7	23
Russia	8	6	8	22

Which country earned the
same number of gold medals
as the United States?   _____

Hint #1:

The United States
earned **9** gold medals.
Which other country
earned the **same**
amount of gold medals?

Hint #2:

Read the chart
carefully!

Answer:

Austria earned the same number of gold
medals as the United States. The **United States**
and **Austria** both earned 9 gold medals.

9. The chart below lists the **zip codes** and **area codes** for 5 places with colorful names.

Use the data from the chart to answer the question.

CITY or TOWN	ZIP CODE	AREA CODE
Green Bay, Wisconsin	54303	920
Orange Park, Florida	32073	904
Bluefield, West Virginia	24701	304
Red Bank, Tennessee	37415	423
Blackwell, Oklahoma	74631	405

What is the **area code** for Orange Park, Florida? _____

Hint #1:
The numbers in the **first column** next to the city or town name list the **zip codes**.

Hint #2:
The numbers in the **second column** next to the city or town name list the **area codes**.

Answer:
The area code for Orange Park, Florida, is **904**.

10. Let's look at our colorful city and town chart one more time!

Read the chart. Use the data from the chart to answer the question.

CITY or TOWN	ZIP CODE	AREA CODE
Green Bay, Wisconsin	54303	920
Orange Park, Florida	32073	904
Bluefield, West Virginia	24701	304
Red Bank, Tennessee	37415	423
Blackwell, Oklahoma	74631	405

Which city or town has the zip code **37415**? **Circle** your answer.

Green Bay, Wisconsin   Red Bank, Tennessee

Bluefield, West Virginia   Blackwell, Oklahoma

Hint #1:
Remember, the numbers in the **first column** next to the city or town name list the **zip codes**.

Hint #2:
The numbers in the **second column** next to the city or town name list the **area codes**.

Answer:
Red Bank, Tennessee , has the zip code 37415.

11. The **pictograph** below shows the number of stars found on 5 different flags that are flown by countries around the world.

Look at the key. Read the pictograph. Then answer the questions on the next page.

Country	Number of Stars on Flag
Panama	☆☆
New Zealand	☆☆☆☆
Iraq	☆☆☆
Venezuela	☆☆☆☆☆☆☆
Honduras	☆☆☆☆☆
Key: ☆ = 1 star on flag	

a) How many stars are on the flag for **Honduras**? **Circle** your answer.

2   3   4   5

b) How many stars on the flag for **Panama**? **Circle** your answer.

2   3   4   5

c) Which country has a flag with **4 stars**? **Circle** your answer.

Panama   New Zealand   Iraq   Venezuela

Hint #1:

Look at the **key**.
Each ☆ represents **1 star** on a country's flag.

Hint #2:

Count the **number of stars** beside the name of each country.

Answer:

a) There are 5 stars on the Honduras flag.

b) There are 2 stars on the Panama flag.

c) New Zealand has a flag with 4 stars.

12. Read the **maximum speed** of the
6 animals on the chart below.

Antelope	Rabbit	Cheetah
60 miles per hour	40 miles per hour	70 miles per hour
Grizzly Bear	Lion	Wild Turkey
30 miles per hour	50 miles per hour	20 miles per hour

Use the data from the chart to create a
pictograph on the next page.

Read the key. Let one ● **equal 10 miles
per hour**.

Animal	Speed (Miles per Hour)
Antelope	
Rabbit	
Cheetah	
Grizzly Bear	
Lion	
Wild Turkey	
KEY: ● = 10 miles per hour	

Hint #1:

Read the **key**. Each ● equals **10 miles per hour**. Count by **10** to make sure that you have drawn the correct number.

Hint #2:

A lion's top speed is **50 miles per hour**. Here is how it would look in the pictograph.

Lion	● ● ● ● ●

Answer: Does your pictograph look like this?

Animal	Speed (Miles per Hour)
Antelope	● ● ● ● ● ●
Rabbit	● ● ● ●
Cheetah	● ● ● ● ● ● ●
Grizzly Bear	● ● ●
Lion	● ● ● ● ●
Wild Turkey	● ●
KEY: ● = 10 miles per hour	

13. Use the **bar graph** to answer the questions below.

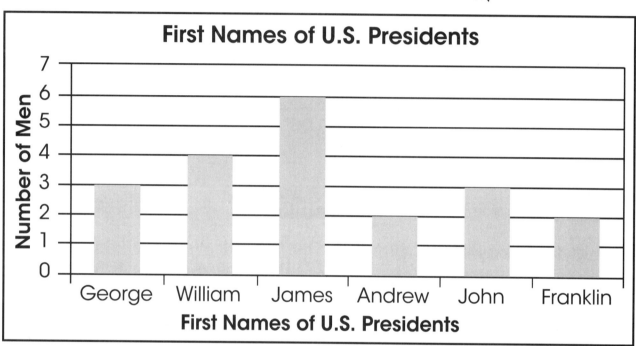

First Names of U.S. Presidents

Number of Men

George William James Andrew John Franklin

First Names of U.S. Presidents

a) How many U.S. presidents were named **William**? **Circle** your answer.

3   4   5   6

b) How many U.S. presidents were named **Franklin**? **Circle** your answer.

2   3   4   5

c) How many U.S. presidents were named **John**? **Circle** your answer.

3   4   5   6

Hint #1:

The **number** on the left of the graph shows you how many U.S. presidents had that name.

Hint #2:

Look at the **name** under each bar on the graph. Place your finger at the top of each bar and drag it to the **left**.

Answer:

a) 4 U.S. presidents were named William.

b) 2 U.S. presidents were named Franklin.

c) 3 U.S. presidents were named John.

14. The **pictograph** below shows the number of days that it rained each month last year.

Read the pictograph. Look at the key. Then answer the questions below.

Month	Number of Days It Rained Last Year
January	◊◊◊
February	◊◊◊
March	◊◊◊
April	◊◊◊
May	◊◊◊◊◊
June	◊◊◊◊◊◊
July	◊◊◊◊◊◊◊
August	◊◊◊◊◊◊◊
September	◊◊◊◊◊◊◊
October	◊◊◊◊◊◊
November	◊◊◊◊
December	◊◊◊
Key: ◊ = 1 day	

a) Which of these months had the **most** days of rain last year? **Circle** the correct answer.

January   May   October   August

© Kaplan Publishing, Inc.

b) Which of these months had the **least** days of rain last year? **Circle** the correct answer.

May   June   November   December

c) Which month had the same number of rainy days as **August**? **Circle** the correct answer.

January   June   July   October

Hint #1:

Read the **key**. Each ⬡ equals **1 day of rain**.

Hint #2:

Look at the data for August.

August	⬡⬡⬡⬡⬡⬡⬡⬡

1 2 3 4 5 6 7 8 =
8 days of rain last year

Answer:

a) August had the most days of rain last year. August had **8 days** of rain last year.

b) December had the least days of rain last year. December had **3 days** of rain last year.

c) July had the same number of rainy days as August. July and August each had **8 days** of rain last year.

15. The chart below shows some **state birds** and the **number of states** having each bird as their state bird.

State Bird	# of States
Eastern Goldfinch	2
Cardinal	7
Chicadee	2
Mockingbird	5
Western Meadowlark	6
Mountain Bluebird	2

Use the data above to fill in the **bar graph** below.

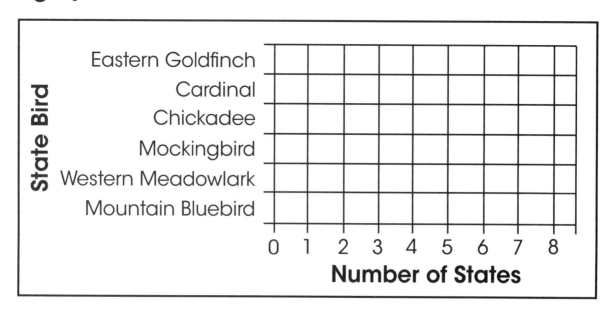

Hint #1:

For each bird, color in the **number of boxes** that matches the **number of states** that each bird represents.

Hint #2:

Here's one to get you started: **2 states** use the **eastern goldfinch** as their state bird. This is how the eastern goldfinch should look in your bar graph.

Eastern Goldfinch	▓	▓						

Answer: Your bar graph should look like this.

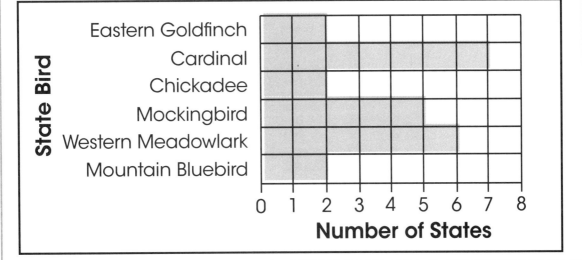

Challenge Activity

You're doing a great job so far!
Are you ready for a Challenge Activity?
Good luck!

Six apples are growing on the **grid** below. Identify the **coordinates** of each apple.

The first one has been done for you.

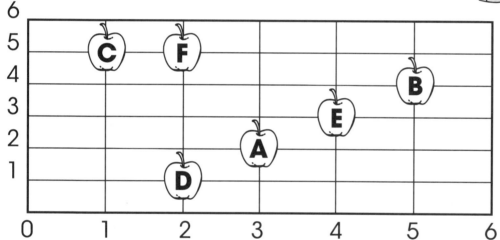

1. Apple A: (3, 2)

2. Apple B: (___ , ___)

3. Apple C: (___ , ___)

4. Apple D: (___ , ___)

5. Apple E: (___ , ___)

6. Apple F: (___ , ___)

Hint #1:

Place your pointer finger on **0**. Move your finger **over** to the **right** until you reach the line that the apple is growing on. This will be the **first number** of the ordered pair.

Hint #2:

Place your finger at the **bottom** of the line that the apple is growing on. Let your finger climb **up** to the apple. This will be the **second number** of the ordered pair.

Answers to Challenge Activity:

1. Apple A: (**3, 2**)   **2.** Apple B: (**5, 4**)

3. Apple C: (**1, 5**)   **4.** Apple D: (**2, 1**)

5. Apple E: (**4, 3**)   **6.** Apple F (**2, 5**)

Let's take a quick test and see how much you've learned during this climb up *SCORE!* Mountain. Good luck!

1. Represent the following numbers using tally marks.

   4: _____

   22: _____

   16: _____

Use the pictograph below to answer questions 2 and 3.

Favorite Pets in Second Grade	
Cat	☐☐☐☐☐☐
Dog	☐☐☐☐☐☐☐☐☐
Hamster	☐☐☐☐☐
Key: ☐ = 1 student	

2. How many students said **dog** was their favorite pet? _____

3. How many more students liked **cats** more than **hamsters**? _____

Use the bar graph below to answer questions 4 and 5.

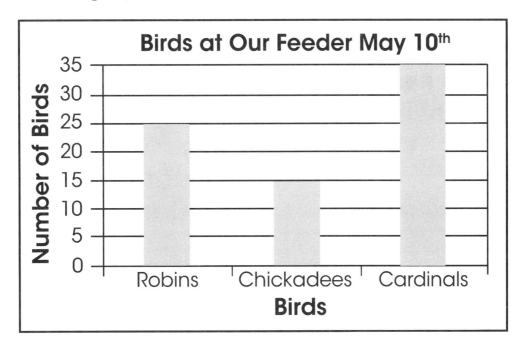

4. How many **chickadees** visited the feeder on May 10th? _____

5. How many more **cardinals** than **robins** visited the feeder on May 10th? _____

Answers to test questions:

1. 4: IIII
22: ⟋⟋⟋⟋ ⟋⟋⟋⟋ ⟋⟋⟋⟋ ⟋⟋⟋⟋ II
16: ⟋⟋⟋⟋ ⟋⟋⟋⟋ ⟋⟋⟋⟋ I

2. Dogs received **10 votes**.

3. Cats received **1 more vote** than hamsters.

4. **15 chickadees** visited the feeder on May 10th.

5. **10** more cardinals than robins visited the feeder on May 10th.

Celebrate!

Let's take a fun break before we go to the next base camp. You've earned it!

Let's make a personal pencil holder!

Here's what you need:

- An empty cardboard cake frosting or raisin can that has been cleaned, washed, and dried

Congratulations! You're almost to the top of *SCORE!* Mountain.

- Double-sided tape (sticky on both sides)
- A sheet of white paper
- Crayons and magic markers in your favorite colors
- Things to decorate your pencil holder, including colored glue and glitter
- Scissors (ask an adult for help with cutting)

Directions:

- Cut your white sheet of paper so that it fits neatly around your empty can. Ask an adult for help with cutting. This will be your pencil holder label!
- Decorate your white sheet of paper any way you want!
- Here are some decorating ideas:
    o Use your favorite colors.
    o Use colored glue and glitter.
    o Draw fun pictures of things that you like.
    o Write your name.
- When you're done decorating your paper, stick it neatly around your can using double-sided tape.

Continued on next page.

- Fill your new personal pencil holder with all of your pencils!

- You can make a pencil holder for home and another for school!

- Show off your creative work to your family and friends.

Good luck and have fun! You deserve it for working so hard!

Base Camp

6

Everyday Math

You've made it to the final base camp! Outstanding! Make it through and you'll be at the top of *SCORE!* Mountain. You can do it! Good luck!

SCORE! MOUNTAIN TOP

BASE CAMP 5

BASE CAMP 4

BASE CAMP 3

BASE CAMP 2

BASE CAMP 1

1. Add the values of the coins.

Record the total value for the coins on the line below.

Value of coins: _____

Hint #1:

= 1¢   = 5¢   = 10¢

Hint #2:

It might help to write down the **sum** as you add each coin.

Answer:

Value of coins: **36 cents**

10¢ + 10¢ + 5¢ + 5¢ + 5¢ + 1¢ = **36¢**

2. Let's look at a few more sets of coins!

a)

Value of coins: _____

b)

Value of coins: _____

Hint #1:

Count carefully!

Hint #2:

It might help to write down the **sum** as you add each coin.

Answer:

a) Value of coins: **42 cents**
25¢ + 10¢ + 5¢ + 1¢ + 1¢ = **42¢**

b) Value of coins: **46 cents**
10¢ + 25¢ + 5¢ + 5¢ + 1¢ = **46¢**

3. Sue Ellen is helping her mom around the house.

Fill in the number value beside the coins that she's earned.

Value: _____ ¢

Hint #1:

Remember, a quarter is worth **25 cents**.

Hint #2:

When the value is **less than a dollar**, you use the cent (¢) symbol.

Answer:

75¢

25¢ + 25¢ + 25¢ = **75¢**

4. Liz has some coins in her pocket.

Read the riddle below. **Circle** the correct group of coins that are in her pocket.

I have **three different coins** in my pocket.
The value of the coins is **31¢**.
Can you guess my coins?

A.

B.

C.

See hints and answer on following page.

Hint #1:

Which answer choice shows coins that are worth a total of **31¢**?

Hint #2:

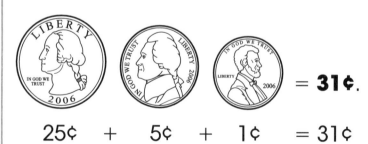

= 1¢   = 5¢

= 10¢   = 25¢

Answer: Choice **B** is correct.

= **31¢**.

25¢   +   5¢   +   1¢   = 31¢

5. Bob has some coins in his pocket, too!

Read the riddle below. **Circle** the correct coins that are in his pocket.

I have **four coins** in my pocket.
Two of the coins are **dimes**.
The value of the coins is **46¢**.
Can you guess my coins?

A.

B.

C.

See hints and answer on following page.

Hint #1:

Remember, Bob has **4 coins** in his pocket.

Hint #2:

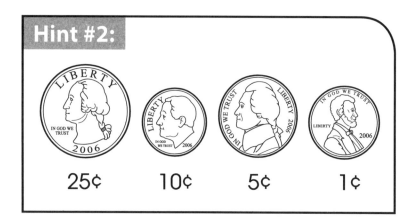

25¢   10¢   5¢   1¢

Answer: Choice **C** is correct.

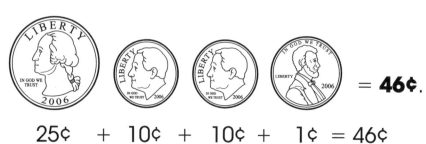 **= 46¢**.

25¢   +   10¢   +   10¢ +   1¢ = 46¢

6. Joseph bought a new ball. The ball costs **24¢**. He gives the clerk **3 dimes**. What will his change be? **Circle** your answer.

7¢   **6¢**   **5¢**   **4¢**

Hint #1:

How much did the ball cost?
How much money did Joseph give to the clerk?

Hint #2:

You may create a **subtraction equation** to find the amount of change that the customer will receive.

Example: 30¢   given to clerk (3 dimes)
                − 24¢   cost of ball
            _____ ¢   change given to customer

Answer:

Joseph gets back 6¢.
30¢ − 24¢ = 6¢

7. Look at the clocks in the boxes below.

Follow the clues, and put an **X** or an **O** in the right box.

1. Place an **X** in the box containing the clock that shows **12:00**.

2. Place an **O** in the box containing the clock that shows **30 minutes past eight**.

Hint #1:

When the time is **12:30**, the minute hand will be pointing to the **6**, and the hour hand will be pointing between the **12** and the **1**.

Hint #2:

When the time is **6:00**, the minute hand will be pointing to the **12**. The hour hand will be pointing directly to the **6**.

Answer: The boxes should look like this:

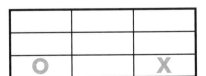

8. Cindy has a very busy week ahead!

She has a **different activity** planned for each of the seven days.

Read the clues below. **Fill in** the activity and the time on the schedule below.

Cindy's Busy Week	
Day	**Activity**
Sunday	
Monday	
Tuesday	
Wednesday	
Thursday	
Friday	
Saturday	

1. I will **get my hair cut** on the **fourth day of the week**.

2. I have a **tennis lesson** on the **day before Friday**.

3. I will **babysit Cole** on the **last day of the week**.

4. **Uncle Quentin will visit** on the **first day of the week**.

5. My **dentist appointment** is on the **day before Wednesday**.

6. I will **walk Catherine's dog** on the **second day of the week**.

7. I will **begin painting the porch** on the **sixth day of the week**.

Hint #1:

Sunday is the **first** day of the week.

Hint #2:

Saturday is the **last** day of the week.

Answer: This is what Cindy's schedule should look like.

Cindy's Busy Week	
Day	**Activity**
Sunday	Uncle Quentin visits
Monday	Walk Catherine's dog
Tuesday	Dentist appointment
Wednesday	Haircut
Thursday	Tennis lesson
Friday	Begin painting the porch
Saturday	Babysit Cole

9. Read the clues on the birthday cakes and **write** the **correct month** below each cake.

a)

John celebrated his birthday in the **first month** of the year.

_____

b)

William celebrated his birthday in the month **after May**.

_____

Hint #1:

The first month of the year is **January**. The last month of the year is **December**.

Hint #2:

It may help to look at a **calendar** to remember the order of the months.

Answer:

John's birthday is in **January**.

William's birthday is in **June**.

10. **Draw** hands on the clocks below to show the time that each runner finished the race.

a) Runner A finished the race at **7:15**.	**b)** Runner B finished the race right at **4:30**.	**c)** Runner C finished the race at **3:45**.

Hint #1:

The **minute hand** is pointing to the **6** when the time is **30 minutes past the hour**.

Hint #2:

Answer: Do your clocks look like these?

a)    **b)**    **c)**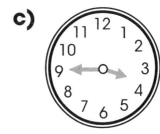

11. Solve the **addition** and **subtraction** problems below to identify some important temperatures!

a) Water freezes at _____ degrees Fahrenheit.
$$(10 + 20 + 2)$$

b) Water boils at _____ degrees Celsius.
$$(25 + 25 + 25 + 25)$$

c) A normal body temperature is about _____ degrees Farenheit.
$$(100 - 2)$$

Hint #1:

Which equations are **addition**? Which equations are **subtraction**?

Hint #2:

Example: $$\begin{array}{r} 100 \\ 100 \\ 10 \\ +2 \\ \hline \textbf{212 degrees} \end{array}$$

Answer:

a) Water freezes at **32 degrees Fahrenheit**.

b) Water boils at **100 degrees Celsius**.

c) A normal body temperature is about **98 degrees Fahrenheit**.

© Kaplan Publishing, Inc.

12. Read the chart of **Roman numerals** below.

I	II	III	IV	V	VI	VII	VIII	IX	X
1	2	3	4	5	6	7	8	9	10

Use the chart to solve these equations.
Write the correct answer in Roman numerals.

a) II + VII = _____

b) IV + IV = _____

c) X − IX = _____

Hint #1:

Read the chart carefully!

Hint #2:

II + VII = 2 + 7 = ?
V + V = 5 + 5 = ?

Answer:

a) II + VII = **IX**
    2 + 7 = 9

b) IV + IV = **VIII**
    4 + 4 = 8

c) X − IX = **I**
    10 − 9 = 1

© Kaplan Publishing, Inc.

13. Let's try some **larger** Roman numerals!

Read the chart of Roman numerals below.

XI	XII	XIII	XIV	XV	XVI	XVII	XVIII	IXX	XX
11	12	13	14	15	16	17	18	19	20

Use the chart to solve these equations.
Write the correct answer in Roman numerals.

a) IX + IX = _____

b) X + X = _____

c) XVII − IX = _____

Hint #1:

Remember to read the chart carefully!

Hint #2:

II + VII = 2 + 7 = ?
V + V = 5 + 5 = ?

Answer:

a) IX + IX = **XVIII**
   9 + 9 = 18

b) X + X = **XX**
   10 + 10 = 20

c) XVII − IX= **VIII**
   17 − 9 = 8

© Kaplan Publishing, Inc.

14. Calling the Animal Kingdom!

Use the numbers below to figure out the value of each of the animals listed.

The first one has been done for you!

1	2 A B C	3 D E F
4 G H I	5 J K L	6 M N O
7 P Q R S	8 T U V	9 W X Y Z
*	0	#

1. D - O - G   3 + 6 + 4 = 13

2. C - A - T   ____ + ____ +____ = ____

3. F - O - X   ____ + ____ +____ = ____

See hints and answers on the following page.

Hint #1:

Look at the **number** above each **letter** of the animal's name. **Add** the three numbers together.

Hint #2:

Make sure you're looking at the right numbers!

Answer:

1. D - O - G: **3 + 6 + 4** = 13

2. C - A - T: **2 + 2 + 8** = 12

3. F - O - X: **3 + 6 + 9** = 18

15. Look at the four directions on the 100 chart below.

To travel **north**, move your finger **up**.

To travel **south**, move your finger **down**.

To travel **east**, move your finger to the **right**.

To travel **west**, move your finger to the **left**.

NORTH ↑

1	2	3	4	5	6	7	8	9	10
11	12	13	14	15	16	17	18	19	20
21	22	23	24	25	26	27	28	29	30
31	32	33	34	35	36	37	38	39	40
41	42	43	44	45	46	47	48	49	50
51	52	53	54	55	56	57	58	59	60
61	62	63	64	65	66	67	68	69	70
71	72	73	74	75	76	77	78	79	80
81	82	83	84	85	86	87	88	89	90
91	92	93	94	95	96	97	98	99	100

WEST ←

EAST →

SOUTH ↓

Read the instructions below. Move your finger along the 100 chart. Identify the number in the box where your finger ends up.

Start at **44**. Take **2** steps **north**. Take **5** steps to the **east**. Take **3** steps **south**.

What number are you pointing to? _____

Hint #1:
Remember, to travel **north**, move your finger **up**. To travel **south**, move your finger **down**.

Hint #2:
Remember, to travel **east**, move your finger to the **right**. To travel **west**, move your finger to the **left**.

Answer:
You should be pointing to **59**.

© Kaplan Publishing, Inc.

You're doing a great job so far! Are you ready for a Challenge Activity? Good luck!

Read the **Candy Town train schedule** below. Use the schedule to answer the questions on the next page. **Circle** your answers.

Stop Number	Stops	Arrival Time	Departure Time
1	Hot Fudge Lake	2:00	2:30
2	Whipped Cream Mountain	3:15	3:45
3	Candy Cane Cottage	4:00	5:15
4	Lollipop Landing	5:30	6:30
5	Fudge Forest	6:45	7:15

a) How long will it take the train to reach **Hot Fudge Lake**?

30 minutes   1 hour   2 hours

b) What time will you arrive at **Whipped Cream Mountain**?

2:30   3:45   3:15

c) Where will you be at **5:45**?

Candy Cane Cottage
Fudge Forest
Lollipop Landing

Answer:

a) It will take the train **1 hour** to reach Hot Fudge Lake.

b) You will arrive at Whipped Cream Mountain at **3:15**.

c) You will be at **Lollipop Landing** at 5:45.

Test

Let's take a quick test and see how much you've learned during this climb up **SCORE!** Mountain. Good luck!

1. What time is it? Circle your answer.

4:00   4:15   4:30   4:45

2. Which months come right before and right after **March**? Write your answers in the squares below.

	March	

3. Which days come right before and right after **Thursday**? Write your answers in the squares below.

	Thursday	

4. **Add** the values of the coins below and write the total.

_____ ¢

5. Fill in the blank.

Water freezes at _____ degrees Fahrenheit.

Answers to test questions:

1. reads **4:15**.

2.

February	**March**	April

3.

Wednesday	**Thursday**	Friday

4.

__53¢__

5. Water freezes at **32 degrees Fahrenheit**.

Celebrate!

Let's have some fun and celebrate your success! You've earned it!

Let's make a friendship card!

Congratulations! You've made it to the top of *SCORE!* Mountain. You did a great job!

SCORE! MOUNTAIN TOP

BASE CAMP 6

BASE CAMP 5

BASE CAMP 4

BASE CAMP 3

BASE CAMP 2

BASE CAMP 1

You will need:

- A piece of white construction paper

- Things to use to decorate your friendship card, including colored glue, pictures, glitter, crayons, and magic markers.

Directions:

- Take your piece of white construction paper and fold it in half to form a card.

- On the front of the card, write the name of the friend to whom you want to give your card.

- On the inside of the card, write a special note to your friend, or draw them a nice picture.

- Decorate your friendship card any way you like using fun colors and drawings.

- When you're finished, give the card to your friend!

- It's a nice way to let a friend know what you think about them!

Have fun! You should be really proud! I knew you could make it to the top!

Here are some helpful tools to guide you through each base camp!

Use these tools whenever you need a helping hand during your climb up *SCORE!* Mountain.

Coins

Measurements

penny – 1¢	nickel – 5¢	dime – 10¢	quarter – 25¢
Heads	Heads	Heads	Heads
Tails	Tails	Tails	Tails

Capacity: 1 cup = 8 ounces
1 pint = 2 cups
1 quart = 2 pints
1 gallon = 4 quarts

Length: 12 inches = 1 foot

Temperature: 32° Fahrenheit → water freezes
100° Celsius → water boils

Days of the Week

Sunday	Monday	Tuesday	Wednesday	Thursday	Friday	Saturday
1st	2nd	3rd	4th	5th	6th	7th

Months of the Year

	Month	Number of Days		Month	Number of Days
1st	January	31	7th	July	31
2nd	February	28/29	8th	August	31
3rd	March	31	9th	September	30
4th	April	30	10th	October	31
5th	May	31	11th	November	30
6th	June	30	12th	December	31

Shapes

A **square** has **4** equal sides and **4** corners.

A **circle** has **0** corners.

A **triangle** has **3** sides and **3** corners.

A **rectangle** has **4** sides, **2** that are longer and **2** that are shorter, and **4** corners.

Geometric Solids

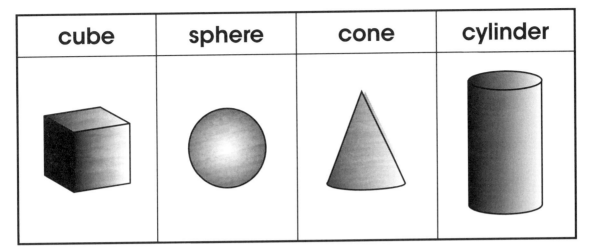

cube	sphere	cone	cylinder

Patterns

Repeating	● ■ ● ■ ● ■ ●
Growing	▲ ▼ ▲ ▼ ▼ ▲ ▼ ▼ ▼

Place Value

356

Hundreds	Tens	Ones
3	5	6

Skip Counting

Twos	2, 4, 6, 8, 10, 12, 14, 16, 18, 20, 22, 24, 26, 28, 30 . . .
Threes	3, 6, 9, 12, 15, 18, 21, 24, 27, 30 . . .
Fives	5, 10, 15, 20, 25, 30, 35, 40, 45, 50, 55, 60 . . .
Tens	10, 20, 30, 40, 50, 60, 70, 80, 90, 100 . . .

Symbols

+	plus (addition)
−	minus (subtraction)
=	equals
<	less than
>	greater than

You can do it!

Use these blank pages to work out the questions in your *SCORE! Mountain Challenge Workbook*.

You can do it!

You can do it!

You can do it!

You can do it!

You can do it!

You can do it!

You can do it!

You can do it!

You can do it!

You can do it!

You can do it!

You can do it!

You can do it!

You can do it!

You can do it!

© Kaplan Publishing, Inc.

You can do it!

You can do it!
No peeking!

SCORE!

Answer Hider

Tear out your answer hider and use it to cover up the answers on the bottom of every page.

Try to come up with the right answers before looking!

Ask an adult for help with cutting.